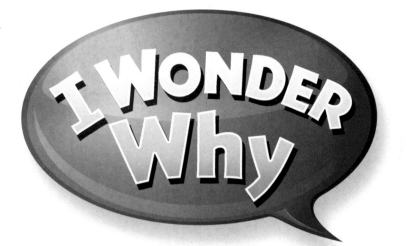

I WONDER Why

Soap Makes Bubbles

and other questions about science

Barbara Taylor

KINGFISHER
NEW YORK

Copyright © Kingfisher 2013
Published in the United States by Kingfisher,
175 Fifth Ave., New York, NY 10010
Kingfisher is an imprint of Macmillan Children's
Books, London.
All rights reserved.

Distributed in the U.S. and Canada by Macmillan,
175 Fifth Ave., New York, NY 10010

Library of Congress Cataloging-in-Publication data
has been applied for.

ISBN: 978-0-7534-6936-1

Kingfisher books are available for special promotions and
premiums. For details contact: Special Markets Department,
Macmillan, 175 Fifth Ave., New York, NY 10010.

For more information, please visit www.kingfisherbooks.com

Printed in China
9 8 7 6 5 4 3 2 1
1TR/0912/UTD/WKT/140MA

Illustrations: Chris Forsey 6–7, 9, 12–13, 14–15, 21, 23, 24–25,
27, 28–29, 30–31; Ruby Green cover, 4–5, 7, 8–9, 16–17,
22–23, 26–27; Tony Kenyon (all cartoons); Biz Hull (Artist
Partners Limited) 10–11, 18–19, 20–21.

CONTENTS

What is science about?

Science is all about discovering how and why things happen in the world around you. It's about everyday things like finding out where water goes when it boils, as well as more complicated things like why we need water to live.

3 Put some water in the freezer, and leave it for an hour or two. What do you notice when you take it out? The water isn't liquid any more—it's a solid, and you can't pour solids.

1 The kitchen is a great place for scientists. Start by turning on a tap and looking at the water that flows out. Runny things like water are called liquids.

2 Now fill a jug with water, and pour it into a cup. Most liquids will pour, but some move faster than others. Try pouring some honey into a saucer—does it move as quickly as water?

What do scientists do?

One of the first things scientists do is ask questions. Then they try to answer the questions by looking closely at things and testing out their ideas. We call this experimenting. Scientists sometimes manage to find the answers—but not always!

4 All liquids can change shape, but most solids can't. Pour some water into a Jell-O pan, and it will fill up all the nooks and crannies. What happens when you put ice cubes in?

5 Ask a grown-up to put a cup of water into a saucepan and boil it for you for five minutes. A lot of steam comes off, doesn't it? Let the water cool, and then pour it back into the cup. There's less water now—where has the rest gone?

6 When water boils, it changes from a liquid into a gas called water vapor. We can't see this gas, so it looks as if the water has disappeared.

What can walk on water?

Tiny insects called water striders are so light that they can walk across water without sinking into it! But even water striders wouldn't get anywhere without a force called surface tension. This pulls on the surface of the water, making a thin, stretchy "skin" on the top.

Raindrops aren't completely round—they're almost flat underneath.

Why are water droplets round?

Small drops of water are almost perfectly round because they are pulled into this shape by surface tension. Bigger drops spread out, though—they're too heavy for surface tension to work as well.

The Jesus Christ lizard runs so fast that it can cross rivers and lakes without sinking—an excellent way to escape from danger!

Gently touch a drop of water with a soapy straw, and watch how the drop gets flatter. This is because soap weakens the surface tension of water—it can no longer pull the drop into a neat round shape.

Why does soap make bubbles?

Adding soap to water weakens the pull of the surface tension, making the surface of the water much stretchier. It spreads out enough for you to blow air inside—a little bit like blowing up balloons with water.

Why do water wings help me float?

When you blow up your water wings, you push a lot of air inside them. Air is much lighter than water, so it helps you float. But the water helps, too, because it pushes up on things. By pushing up on your water wings, it keeps you floating on the surface.

It's easier to float in salty seawater than in freshwater. The Dead Sea in the Middle East is the world's saltiest sea—swimmers can't sink in it, even without water wings!

Experiment with floating and sinking by finding five things that are light enough to float and five that sink because they are too heavy.

Divers don't want to float. To help them sink, they wear a belt with heavy weights on it—not something you should try!

Many fish have a bag of air called a swim bladder inside of them. It works a little like a water wing. When fish fill the bladder with air, they float high up in the water. When they let the air out, they float lower down.

Why do sharks have to keep swimming?

If sharks stop swimming, they sink like stones. This is because they are heavy for their size, and they don't have swim bladders. They have to keep swimming to stay up in the ocean, just like you have to swim or tread water.

Why do I run out of energy?

When you run, the stored energy in your body is changed into movement energy.

You run out of energy because you use it! Walking, running, and jumping all need energy—without it you wouldn't be able to talk, write, read, or even sleep! Energy is stored inside your body and comes from your food. That's why you get hungry—your body is telling you to put back some of the energy you've used.

A lot of things give out energy in many different forms. Here are just a few of them.

Fire = heat energy

Bike = movement energy

Drum = sound energy

Eating a small apple gives you enough energy to sleep for half an hour.

Energy is never made or destroyed. It just changes from one form to another. Bending a bow stores energy in the bow. This changes into movement energy as the arrow flies from the bow.

What is energy?

Energy makes things happen—nothing in the universe would work without it. You can't see energy, but you can see what it does to things around you. Because of energy, cars move and planes fly, lamps give off light, drums make music, and fires provide heat.

Food = chemical energy

Train = electrical energy

Flashlight = light energy

Why does the spoon get hot when I stir my cocoa?

 Heat energy never keeps still. It is always moving. The spoon warms up when you stir your cocoa because heat energy is moving from the hot drink into the spoon.

Things that allow heat to pass through them easily are called conductors. A metal spoon is a good conductor.

Our bodies give off heat all the time. Some burglar alarms work by picking up the heat given off by a burglar's body.

Why is sunlight warm?

Sunlight is warm because the Sun gives off heat as well as light energy. The Sun's heat energy travels toward us in invisible straight lines called heat rays. You can't see them, of course, but you can feel them on your skin on hot sunny days.

You get cold feet when you stand on a tiled floor because the tiles carry heat energy away from them. Your feet feel warmer on a carpet because it doesn't carry heat away as well as the tiles do.

How do hang gliders hitch rides?

When the Sun heats the land, the land then warms the air above it. Warm air is lighter than cold air, and it rises up into the sky. Hang gliders use this rising warm air to help them fly. The rising currents of warm air are called thermals.

How do divers stay warm?

The problem with heat energy moving around is that it sometimes makes it difficult to stay warm. Divers usually wear rubber wet suits in cold water because rubber doesn't conduct heat well—it stops body heat from escaping as quickly as it would normally. Things that don't carry heat energy well are called insulators.

Jackets lined with down (a duck's soft, warm feathers) keep you cozy in cold weather. Warm air is trapped between the feathers in the jacket and held next to your body.

Beneath their skin, seals have a thick layer of fat called blubber. This insulates their bodies and helps keep them warm in the coldest oceans.

A thin layer of water is trapped between the rubber wet suit and the diver's body. The diver's own body heat warms the water, and the rubber wet suit stops the heat from escaping too quickly.

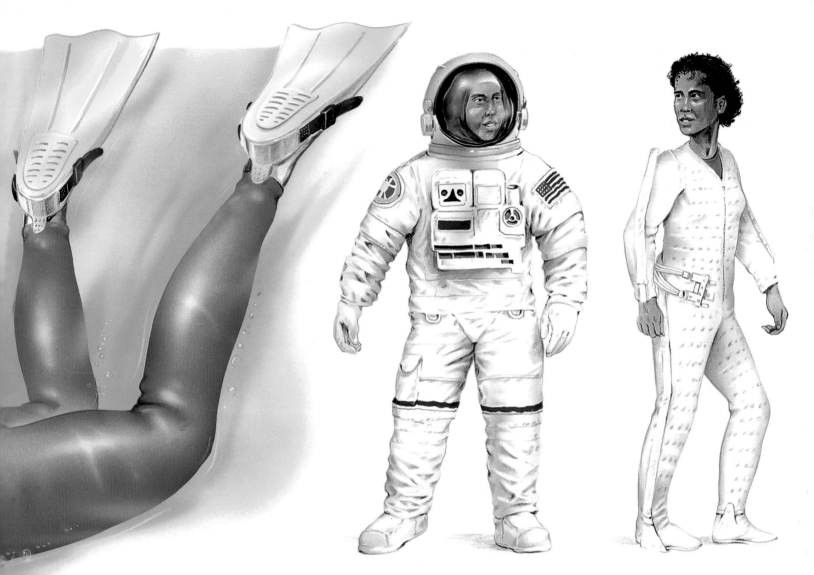

How do astronauts stay cool?

The Sun's rays are much stronger out in space, so astronauts need special ways of staying cool. Under their space suits, they wear a suit of stretchy underwear, kind of like long johns. Tiny plastic tubes run through the underwear, carrying cool water. The water takes away the astronauts' body heat and helps keep them cool.

The space shuttle needed to stay cool, too! Special tiles insulated the shuttle and kept it from getting too hot.

Frying pan handles are made of good insulators. If they weren't, they'd get too hot and burn your hand!

15

Why do I feel cold after a shower?

Your body is always giving off heat. When you're wet, your body heat turns some of the water on your skin into the gas water vapor. This change from a liquid to a gas is called evaporation. You begin to shiver after a shower because evaporation uses up heat.

When you dry your hair with a blow-dryer, you are heating up the water in your hair until it evaporates.

What makes bathroom mirrors steam up?

After a shower, the air in the bathroom is warm and steamy. When it hits a cold surface such as a mirror, the air cools down and changes back into tiny water droplets. These then steam up the mirror. The change from a gas into a liquid is called condensation.

After a chilly night, you may see tiny drops of dew sparkling on spiders' webs or on the grass. Dew comes from water vapor in the air. If air cools down enough during the night, water vapor condenses to form dew.

Condensation is a real problem for dentists. When your warm breath condenses on a mirror, it fogs it up and stops the dentist from being able to see inside your mouth!

17

What is sound?

Sound is a type of energy. It happens when something shakes or moves back and forth really quickly. The shaking movements are called vibrations. You hear sounds because vibrations travel through the air into your ears.

Some singers can sing a note that is so high and so loud that it can break a glass!

Here's a way to watch how sounds vibrate. Tie a piece of thread to some tissue paper. Now, put on some loud music, and hold the thread in front of a loudspeaker. The vibrations should make the tissue paper shake. If they don't, turn up the music!

Crashing a pair of cymbals together makes them vibrate, sending out ringing sounds.

Why do trumpeters blow raspberries?

Blowing raspberries is the only way to get sounds out of a trumpet! It makes a trumpeter's lips vibrate, and this makes the air inside the trumpet shake, too. The air comes out of the other end as a musical note!

Sound travels through the air at 1,115 ft./s (340m/s) —almost the length of four football fields.

Can sound travel under water?

Yes, it can! Sound moves four times faster through water than through air. It can travel such long distances that whales can hear each other when they are more than 60 mi. (100km) apart.

Sound needs something to travel through—air, water, or some other material. There's no air in space, so astronauts have to use radios to talk to one another.

What causes shadows?

Light travels in straight lines called rays. When the rays hit something that they can't shine through, the light is blocked, and a dark shadow forms on the other side.

There are many things that light can't shine through—walls, furniture, your own body, for example. We call these things opaque.

Try to make animal shadows on a wall by wiggling your fingers in the beam of a bright flashlight.

Light is another kind of energy. Plants use the energy in sunlight to make food for themselves in their leaves. Sunflowers get all the sunlight they can by turning to face the Sun as it moves across the sky.

You can use shadows to tell the time. On a sunny day, stick a thread reel to a piece of cardboard and stand a pencil inside of it. Every hour, draw a line along the pencil's shadow, and write down the time. Whenever it's sunny, you can put the cotton-reel clock in the same place, the same way up, and use it to tell the time.

Why can I see through glass?

You can see through glass because it's transparent—that means it's clear, and it lets light shine through. Glass is great for windows because it lets sunlight into a room, allowing you to see what's going on in the world outside!

Bathroom windows are often made out of frosted glass. This still lets some light in, but the frosting stops people outside from seeing straight through the glass.

Can light bounce?

When rays of light hit something that they can't shine through, they bounce off of it—just like a ball bouncing off the ground. This is called reflection. We are able to see things because light is reflected off of them into our eyes.

You can see yourself when you look down into a puddle because the smooth water reflects the light right back into your eyes.

Up periscope! A submarine officer looks through a periscope to see what's happening above the water. Mirrors inside the periscope reflect light from things above the water right down into the officer's eyes.

The Moon reflects light from the Sun. It has no light of its own.

See what happens when light passes through a single drop of water. Cut a hole in a piece of cardboard, and stick scotch-tape over the top. Carefully put a drop of water on the tape, and look through it at something small, like a ladybug. It will make it look bigger.

Why do my legs look shorter under water?

When light enters water, its rays travel more slowly than they do through the air. This changes the way we see things. Looking down through the water in a swimming pool, your legs look very short and stubby. Don't worry— they aren't really!

As light passes through water, it changes the way we see things. This makes it difficult to net fish—they aren't where they appear to be. To catch one, you have to aim below the place where you actually see it.

Why do rainbows happen?

Although sunlight looks white, it's really made out of many different colors. During a shower of rain, sunlight sometimes shines through the tiny raindrops falling through the air. When this happens, the water makes the light spread into all its different colors. The colors always appear in the same order, and a beautiful rainbow forms in the sky.

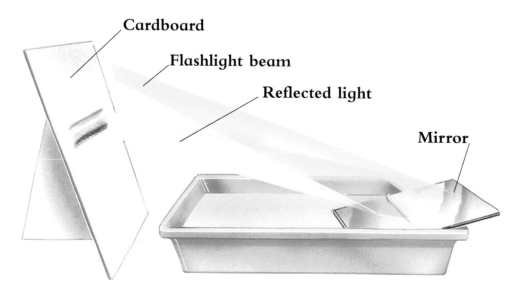

Cardboard

Flashlight beam

Reflected light

Mirror

Another way to see a rainbow is to hold a mirror in a shallow pan of water. Try to bounce sunlight or a flashlight off the mirror onto a piece of white cardboard. The water should make the light spread out into a rainbow.

You don't have to wait for rain to see a rainbow. Water the yard on a sunny day, and you may see rainbow colors in the spray.

Why is grass green?

We see things when light reflects off of them into our eyes. But not all of white light's colors are reflected. Some are soaked up. Grass looks green because it soaks up all the colors in white light apart from green.

The bright colors of many animals often work as a warning. The black and yellow stripes on a wasp warn us—and other animals—to stay away from its poisonous stinger.

Can cats see in color?

Many animals don't really need to see in color. They rely much more on their sharp hearing and sense of smell.

Yes, they can—but they don't see all the colors that you do! Cats don't really need to see the bright colors, as most of them are busiest during the night, outdoors hunting for food.

What is air made of?

Air is a mixture of gases—mostly nitrogen and oxygen with a little bit of carbon dioxide and some water vapor. It also has tiny particles of salt, dust, and dirt. You can't see, smell, or taste the air, but you can feel it when the wind blows.

We don't notice it, but the air around us is heavy and pushes down on us. The air in a medium-sized room weighs as much as 70 cans of beans!

You're using air when you take a deep breath to blow out the candles on a birthday cake!

How do bubbles get into soft drinks?

The bubbles in soft drinks are made out of carbon dioxide. The gas is pushed into the bottle so hard that it disappears into the liquid. When the bottle is opened, the bubbles have room to escape and start fizzing into the air.

Make your own bubbles of carbon dioxide gas by adding a teaspoon of baking powder to a jug of water. Stand by for the fizzing!

Why do cakes rise?

When you put a cake in the oven, the batter heats up and makes bubbles of carbon dioxide. These grow bigger in the heat, causing the cake to rise.

The air you beat into cake batter also helps make the cake deliciously light.

Why do bikes have tires?

As a tire rolls along, it rubs against the road. This rubbing creates a slowing force called friction that helps the tires grip.

Tires help a bike grip the road safely. Look closely at a tire, and you will see that it is patterned. This pattern is called the tread. In wet weather, water escapes from under the tire through the grooves in the tread, stopping your bike from skidding.

Why are tires full of air?

Pumping air into bicycle tires makes them bouncy. They are like a cushion between the wheel and the road, rolling easily over all the bumps and giving you a much smoother ride.

How do bike brakes work?

When you squeeze your bike's brake handles, brake pads press in and grip each wheel. The pads and wheels rub against each other, causing friction that slows the wheels down. Squeeze the brake handles tightly, and your bike will stop completely!

Brake pad

Brake pad

Tread

It's hard work pumping up a tire. You have to squeeze a lot of air into a very small space.

Without friction, we would slip and slide every time we tried to walk! It would be like sliding on banana peels all the time.

Why do we need air?

All animals on Earth need to breathe the oxygen in air to stay alive—and that includes you! That's because bodies use oxygen to make energy for living and growing.

All plants need air, light, and water to live and grow. So do people and every other living thing on our planet.

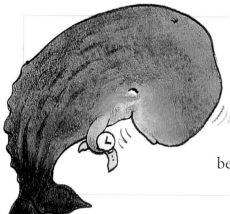

Even though they live in the ocean, whales breathe oxygen from the air. Sperm whales can hold their breath for up to two hours before coming up for air.

Why do we need light?

Without the Sun's light, there would be nothing to eat! Plants are the only living things that can make their own food, and they need sunlight to do this. Everything else on Earth feeds on plants or on plant-eating animals. If there weren't any plants, we'd all starve to death!

If you've ever been camping, you know that the grass beneath a tent turns pale and begins to die. This is because it can't get the sunlight it needs to stay alive. Don't worry—it quickly recovers!

Why do we need water?

It's difficult to imagine, but more than two thirds of your body is made up of water. And the same goes for most other animals and plants. All living things on Earth need water to stay alive. Without it, they would die.

You can survive for many weeks without food. But without water, you'd last just three or four days.

Index